D0629870

momma loves her
some eggnog

Other Books by MikWright

hey, girl!

happy birthday . . .
blah, blah, blah

who's your daddy?

your mother looks good . . .

MikWright . . . family style

mixed nuts

drinks well with others

don't blame me, sister

momma loves her some eggnog

happy holidaze

MikWright

**Andrews McMeel
Publishing, LLC**
Kansas City

08 09 10 11 TWP 10 9 8 7 6 5 4 3 2

ISBN-13: 978-0-7407-6877-4
ISBN-10: 0-7407-6877-8

Library of Congress Control Number:
2007924466

www.andrewsmcmeel.com
www.mikwright.com

Authors' photos by Jason Kinney

ATTENTION: SCHOOLS AND BUSINESSES
Andrews McMeel books are available at quantity
discounts with bulk purchase for educational,
business, or sales promotional use. For
information, please write to: Special Sales
Department, Andrews McMeel Publishing, LLC,
4520 Main Street, Kansas City, Missouri 64111.

We dedicate this compilation
of holiday mayhem to our parents,
Norman and Leona; Weston and Barbara.
Your attempts to keep the season
bright have given us a lifetime of
cherished memories. We love you!

Tim and Phyllis

Cheese cubes, beanie-weenies,
room-temperature bagged shrimp,
and boxed wine (none of which
make for silent nights).

Just get me through this holiday in one piece!

Put down the cell phone,
turn off the laptop, and take
a break from the holidaze. You
are sure to find yourself remi-
niscing about the good old days
when regifting was a thing of
the future.

Peace.
And to all a MikWright!

i'll be home for christmas.

(and in therapy by new year's)

dear santa,

here's a picture of our
chimney. please e-mail me
the dimensions of your ass,
because i don't think this
is gonna work.

love,
emily

momma loves her

some eggnog!

finish up that dry turkey
and we'll go burn one.

does this turkey make
my butt look big?

hey! remember what you gave
me last year for christmas?
well, the cream finally
cleared it up.

holidays with the family are
always a trip . . .
a trip to the liquor store.

so i called mavis to tell
her i got eight inches
last night and, of course,
the bitch claimed
she got nine.

oh, and santa, i would also
like a pink dinette set,
a u-bake-it kitchen, and
some white go-go boots
for my g.i. joe.

this year i've decided
to spend the holidays with
friends. my uncle is really
sick, so i'll save on the
airfare and see the family
at his funeral.

remember the office christmas
party when dottie got so
plastered?

f.y.i. the baby's three months
old and strongly favors floyd
from accounting.

i'm sorry santa.
it "felt" like just a fart.

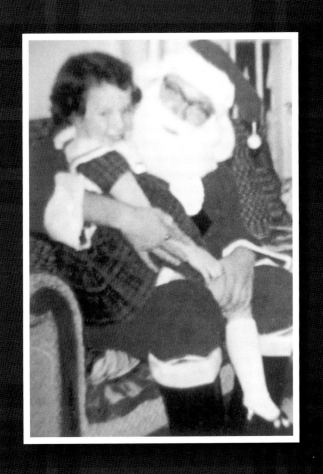

and just then jesus
appeared and said . . .

"hey, kid, it's my birthday
and that's my puppy!"

all i want for christmas is
my two front teeth . . .
ouch! make that a thumb and
a ring finger.

excuse me, santa.
kent gets a wood-burning set,
a tractor trailer rig,
an etch-o-sketch, blue jeans,
and a card game?

well . . . i've been screwed again,
    only this time by a stick pony.

i ran into so many pricks
that day i thought i was
home for the holidays.

every year during the
holidays it's nice to just
relax and have a cocktail.
and then, after the
holidays, it's nice to just
relax and have a cocktail.

seven swans a swimming,

six geese a laying . . .

(make that 3 geese a laying)

where's it written that our kids should be better off than us?

i'm not one to gossip,
but . . . while in
the restroom, i couldn't
help noticing not
everything is small
on an elf.

who's gonna tell
santa about prancer?

let me say three words about
your twig on a card table . . .

white
trash
christmas.

christmas is . . .
by ronnie collins.
well, there was joseph and
mary, and, then, um, some
reindeer flew off with three
wise guys, and the grinch
stole jesus.
can i open my presents now?!

it's sort of the one i
wanted. but hell, i can
always regift it.

from my house to yours . . .
can't you do something
about your hair?

the kids? out back playing
with their new empty boxes.

(whatever it is, i just
hope it fits in my wallet
or my liquor cabinet.)

happy holidays everyone!
kent is now eleven and still
wets the bed. danny turns
eight in january and is
failing remedial math class.
timmy, our six-year-old,
only answers to "jessica."

'twas the night
before christmas and
grandma was smashed.

and now back to
our top story . . .
authorities are still
searching for the baby
jesus snatched from the
nativity scene adjacent to
carl's christmas tree
farm on route 6, now open
from 5 'til 11 p.m. daily
through december 24th.

although a miracle,
mary regretted not
having an epidural.

monica, dear, there
is no santa. now, be a
sweetheart and fix mommy
another martini.

not sure what to get
me for christmas?
i could always use a few
more knick-knacks.

i ain't got no list, santa.
but, could you bring
mama a complete set of
teeth, a veg-o-matic,
and a fifth of vodka?

now sweetheart, i'm only
saying that your sister
shouldn't spend so much on
the kids when she could
be using that money on
electrolysis.

i love it!
(what is it?)

it's perfect!
(what were they thinking?)

it's just what i wanted!
(i hope they saved
the receipt!)

happy holidaze!